CW01498197

Where
Urban
Lights
Reflect
Hope

The Homeless Poet

Printed edition:
Also available in multiple e-book formats.

Published by:
Unheard Voices
An imprint of The Endless Bookcase Ltd
Suite 14 STANTA Business Centre, 3 Soothouse Spring,
St Albans, Hertfordshire, AL3 6PF, UK.

More information can be found at:
www.theendlessbookcase.com

Copyright © 2024 The Homeless Poet
All rights reserved.

ISBN: 978-1-917061-10-0

Where Urban Lights Reflect Hope
Supported using public funding by the National Lottery
through Arts Council England

To my daughter Tiannah
and my brother Lance

The Homeless Poet

From my adolescence, I have harboured a soaring enthusiasm and unremitting compulsion to create poetry/narratives/stories inspired by themes of personal experience and myriad encounters alongside the love of literature and varying genres of music. My overarching objective was to construct short and concise pieces of writing to ignite unease and joy in simultaneous fashion in the minds of readers. To achieve this goal, and develop as a competent poet is the only true occupation of soul I endeavour in perseverance, fortitude and hardship to aspire. Thoughts and ideas to craft worded landscapes manifest themselves at any given time too, and are a reminder that I feel I possess a legitimate right to call myself a poet.

After leaving school, without formal qualifications, I drifted into the employment realm of work taking various jobs in hotels and holiday camps to live-in caring positions with the disabled and elderly to a nomadic gardening role. In more recent years, the shoeshine industry provided my living interspersed by periods of attending college to try and acquire basic academic certificates in differing subjects. But writing poems/narratives/stories always maintained a constant anchor regardless of circumstances entailing lengthy periods of street homelessness and unemployment. Articles written during this time were submitted for newsletters produced by homeless shelters and Christian churches, and once published gave an incentive to see how far I could succeed with my creations in other publications.

One success was joining The Big Issue writing group in the 1990's and seeing poems and stories printed on a monthly basis. It gave meaning and foundation to a peripatetic lifestyle. I did not want to be committed to a permanent home or walk a nine-to-five career path, and readily accepted the place my conscience led. Now older and wiser, my attitude has changed, and I would like to contribute to society through my artistic efforts and feel a sense of purposeful function especially as a light to my daughter. Enduring street life is tough, and adapting to the situation when I initially became homeless has been transformative and nurtured a healthier perspective on society and people. I believe it was a cruel destiny, and a narrative I needed to find a real home.

Contents

The Homeless Poet

Where Urban Lights
Reflect Hope

The Knife

Cutting and tearing,
seeing the sharp blade glisten in warm streetlight,

fighting and stabbing,
knowing a severe wounding will incapacitate might.

Screaming and falling,
streaming blood rushing from sliced vein sparks fear,

pumping and oozing,
escaping liquid fading a cacophonous ambience near.

Bleeding and dripping,
spreading silent crimson venturing across concrete,

burning and dying,
disappearing light flickers death on stationary feet.

Shadows and darkness,
gasping for breath before mortality takes a stake,

death and eternity,
life curtailed by impetuous decisions fool's take.

The knife.

Strand 2024

Strand,
blade displayed,

Strand,
homeless blood afraid.

Strand,
threatening intent replayed,

Strand,
dangerous escalating situation,

Strand,
showing bravado increases retaliation,

Strand,
physical prowess vulnerable to mutilation.

Strand,
trivial words traded, indicate pride must remain,

Strand,
weakness sensed means enactment of serious pain,

Strand,
standing strong with real violence igniting is foolish gain.

Strand,
diplomacy signals the only way for curtailing harmful intent,

Strand,
streetlife represents volatile individuals whose lives are spent,

Strand.
brutalised entities living warped hand-to-mouth accept as meant.

Strand.

Homeless 2024

Homeless,
hostile words traded,

homeless,
confident manner degraded.

Homeless,
skipping handout queue the offence,

homeless,
pathetic underlying situation growing tense.

Homeless,
pride at stake as insulted seeks violent solution,

homeless,
fearful reaction ripe for exploitation in crying destitution.

Homeless,
scarred fists strike with speed at exposed cheekbone,

homeless,
a hard punch surrenders to shooting pain unknown.

Homeless,
falling upon concrete wanting instant retaliation,

homeless,
feeling vulnerable as blood drips anticipation.

Homeless,
physical onslaught employs brutal force,

homeless,
fellow lowlife watch fight they endorse.

Homeless,
psychotic attack charges unabated,

homeless,
beating shows cruelty unrelated.

Homeless.

Child of our Times

Street homeless, neglected child,
raggedly dressed, subject reviled.
Concealed confusion, forlorn state,
system reject, twisted, cruel fate.

Tortured reality, jettisoned dreams,
desecrated spirit, seditious screams.
Impoverished mindset, bleeding soul,
loveless existence, barbarous role.

Ruinous destitution, incarcerated heart,
haunting memories, ripping apart.
Peripatetic wanderings, journeying nowhere,
socially ostracised, gnawing prayer.

Passive begging, survival necessity,
stumbling pleas, exposed vulnerability.
Frightened eyes, enhanced expectation,
stranger's coins, raw compensation.

Sheltering doorways, resentment alight,
hope evaporated, society's blight.
Ravaged years, crushing resignation,
God's unforgotten, awaiting salvation.

Dismissed statistic, accepted fact,
ignored innocence, kindness lacked.
City's embarrassment, callousness rife,
dangerous companions, unending strife.

Child of our times.

Sleep

Teardrops fall from a thousand eyes
and wash homeless streets clean of filth,
of blood, of desperate cries rendered silent
as dreams of harbouring a life dissipates slowly.
Now darkness radiates where living is seen as little
more than disposable like dirty needles lying in greasy
puddles of purifying water reflecting minds of drug-addled
addicts finding oblivion in substances nightmares are created.
Speak not of this if you abide in light, there are sufficient numbers
crying for the broken. All you have to do is close your eyes, then sleep.

Cardboard Boxes

Souls in cardboard boxes...
Why are they hiding inside?
Is it out of desperation
or by pure choice?

Souls in cardboard boxes...
Are they inside through their own fault
or is the blame attributed to society at large?
Should the benevolence of charity assist
or the states' legal structure create a charge?

Unlike the Good Samaritan,
a majority of people choose to walk on the other side.
Individuals who are content to debate lofty moral issues
until reality forces the hypocrites to stumble, fumble, slide and collide.

Rain

Rain,
watery bullets pelting the wet spraying street,

rain,
human body sheltering in cold doorway retreat.

Rain,
saturated pavements reflecting a homeless being,

rain,
public feet splashing past their fixed eyes unseeing.

Rain,
puddles spreading quickly across entrance threshold,

rain,
heavier showers falling indicate sleepless hours unfold.

Rain,
angular shooting arrows strike huddled figure confined,

rain,
temporary haven futile as cascading elements are aligned.

Rain,
crystal baubles pepper open front splattering personal gear,

rain,
lone sodden survivor watches racing rivulets suddenly appear.

Rain,
beautiful overflowing heavens curtail all plans of acquiring respite,

rain,
harsh rainy weather exposes destitutions' forever cruel, cutting plight.

Rain.

Home

How can the saying 'Home is where the heart is'

be applied to individuals sleeping in doorways, church porches and
parks? Not everybody has a physical roof over their heads as

my home is ever shifting and ever moving.

I live through all the seasons but

the weather never improves.

My home remains the concrete pedestrians walk, they keep looking
forward while I always watch my back. My home is not a place of
residence, a place seldom settled, with privacy, comfort or electricity.

Somebody like me just lives each day,

and society says it is a waste.

Lost

People who see me
believe I must be cold,
they cannot ever visualise
the protection of numb pain.

People who see me
think I must feel shame,
they do not realise I am past
caring or bothered about living.

People who see me
look away out of guilt,
they think I should not be
a homeless befallen entity.

People who see me
know life is probably tough.
Danger resides on the streets
and waking up is never guaranteed.

Frozen

Frozen,
concrete stairs permeate,

frozen,
falling temperatures exacerbate.

Frozen,
shivering throughout exposed night,

frozen,
insomnia thwarts the beauty of respite.

Frozen,
staying warm rendered impossible feeling,

frozen,
sharp winter tentacles bring pain in revealing.

Frozen,
thin sleeping bags offer almost no protection,

frozen,
homeless deaths reflect a fearful connection.

Frozen,
lying awake counting crawling hours ahead,

frozen,
imprisoned in a never-ending cycled dread.

Frozen,
suicidal thoughts run through quiet despair,

frozen,
paranoia indicates a life knowing nowhere.

Frozen.

Aliens

Aliens,
strange beings living on the street,

aliens,
odd specimens passed by hasty feet.

Aliens,
wary forms searching for understanding,

aliens,
unknown entities treated with cold handling.

Aliens,
otherworldly species seeking safety to reside,

aliens,
confused creatures abused in a society denied.

Aliens,
planetary bodies wanting accepted rights of light,

aliens,
urban invaders authorities view as a blinding blight.

Aliens,
vulnerable terrestrials enduring hostility at every turn,

aliens,
space warriors lost between two worlds where lives burn.

Aliens,
sentient humanoids hoping compassion arises earthbound,

aliens,
legitimate inhabitants' ensnared reality on abandoned ground.

Aliens.

Homeless Hate

Homeless hate,
frequently spat at,

homeless hate,
visualised street rat.

Homeless hate,
violent proclamations pour,

homeless hate,
condemnatory attitudes claw.

Homeless hate,
belligerent police provoke,

homeless hate,
authorities wantonly stoke.

Homeless hate,
arbitrary arrests made,

homeless hate,
malicious charges laid.

Homeless hate,
system's vulnerable brutalised,

homeless hate,
callous indifference exercised.

Homeless hate,
societal threatening intent,

homeless hate,
disenfranchised lives rent.

Homeless hate, homeless hate, homeless hate.

The Real Request

I was a person until you chose
to explode my myth by ignoring my existence.
I wonder if it was something I said or did I ask too much too loudly?
You were one of many people walking past
too afraid to smile and give money to a stranger.

I am a person and I acknowledged you
please do not harden your heart to me when
I made the concerted effort to soften my heart for you,
it would take you seconds to acknowledge me.

If you choose to pass me, then walk on by,
but please, do not deny my existence!

The Real Request 2

Paralysed by inertia, broken by complacency,
deceived by platitudes, shaken by change, scorned by society,
the people march in procession past another disenfranchised beggar
dependent on other's sympathetic inclinations and kindly acts.

The hours remain indeterminate and indeterminable
for a beggar whose existence passes into accepted mundanity,
and striking hardship between the gutters of futile time.

Loneliness envelops every part of his day
in the populated capital where money dictates,
and people shun the lowest echelons of society.

The sight of such a destitute figure amongst so much opulence
is treated with suspicion, fear, or indifference as comprehension
does not present a reasonable explanation to those in working lives.

Another day now passes before the beggar
with the occasional odd coin thrown in his paper cup,
by individuals all too familiar at the shabby presence
and societal failures to provide for all.

Homeless Entangled Futility

Entangled
within
homeless
bewilderment
and
jettisoned
by
a
hypercritical
Christian
society
for
lying
outside
accepted
parameters,
that
determine
conventional
conduct.
Leaves
no
entrance
for
a
destitute
non-entity
whose
rationale
does
not
correspond
to
the
tune
of
the
resigned

majority.
All
that
remains,
appears
street
survival
where
confusion
and
hatred
conspire
in
equal
measure.

Homeless London

Homeless
and
Ostracised
and
Marginalised
and
Excluded
in
London
while
Each
day
Striving
for
Strength
to
Live
right
On
a
Note
that
Draws
respect
Only
from
Nurtured
perseverance.

Shelter

Shelter,
disingenuous assistance displayed.

Shelter,
bittersweet reassurance conveyed.

Shelter,
virulent realisation dawning.

Shelter,
hated potential warning.

Shelter,
desperation gripping.

Shelter,
morale stripping.

Shelter,
homeless blow.

Shelter,
retributory low.

Shelter,
shattered same.

Shelter,
sought blame.

Shelter,
blind delusion.

Shelter,
felt exclusion.

Shelter,
a curtailed realty.

Shelter.

The Dosser

A
blight
on
the
streets
for
wealthy
tourists
to
witness,
seeing
him
slumped
in
a
shop
doorway
or
lying
on
a
park
bench
watching
society's
blessed
and
privileged
meander
past
indifferent
to
whether
he
lives
or
dies.
And

the
majority
of
these
people
would
consider
themselves
good
Christians
with
caring
predilections.
Hypocrites
if
you
ask me.

The Pavement Artist

You Walk All Over My Picture Of Peace,
You Kick The Chalks All Over The Street,
You Give Me Nothing.

How Can I Draw This Picture Beautifully?

I Don't Gather Inspiration From Insult
Whilst I Retrieve The Chalks To Continue This Picture.

Please Consider,
I Could Have Earned More In Two Minutes Begging
Than I've Made In Two Days Drawing This Picture Of Peace.

Do I Really Have To Sit Here Holding Out My Hand,
Begging For Change Before I Witness a Little Respect?

I Drew a Beautiful Picture,
You Gave Me a Look Of Contempt
Before Throwing a Few Derisory Coins,
And Walking Over My Creation of inspiration.

Beggars

Beggars,
sitting beside ATM machines,

beggars,
playing out constructed themes.

Beggars,
asking strangers for ready cash,

beggars,
hoping money is given in a dash.

Beggars,
avoiding major eye contact,

beggars,
forcing conscience to react.

Beggars,
watching notes being dispersed,

beggars,
pretending indifference acts first.

Beggars,
feeling injustice when denied,

beggars,
deceptive front maintains pride.

Beggars,
avoiding seeking confrontation,

beggars,
determination drives motivation.

Beggars,
waiting until largesse gives,

beggars,
daily routine forever relives.

Beggars.

Destitution

Physical
and
mental
anguish
form
the
foundations
of
destitution
if
the
acquisition
of
money
is
not
achieved
through
viable
means.

The
street
homeless
reside
in
the
accepted
sphere
of
destitution
and
even
choose
this
form
of
penance

as
a
lifestyle unattached
to
responsibility and
leaving
a
minimal carbon
footprint.

Permanence

Permanence,
darkness befalls skeletal trees,

permanence,
winter exacerbates lonely unease.

Permanence,
Regent's Park encroaching embrace,

permanence,
peripheral vagrant's society can displace.

Permeance,
shimmering Metropolis lights start to reflect,

permanence,
inside a distilled realm two feel a real disconnect.

Permanence,
surrounding dying greenery exposes hard mindset,

permanence,
contented souls seen as dystopian live without regret.

Permanence,
repetitious daily drudgery turns the page of each decade,

permanence,
philosophical fortitude embraces open outlook spirit's relay.

Permanence.

(For Nick and Pascal)

I can't Breathe

With his windpipe being crushed by the knee of an over-officious
police officer, a man of different skin tone gasps "I can't breathe".

I can't breathe,
words never to be extinguished.

I can't breathe,
words stamped upon human conscience.

I can't breathe,
words paraded high through ordinary streets.

I can't breathe,
words castigating prevalent, authoritarian brutality.

I can't breathe,
words assailing a shameless state's ethnic supremacy.

I can't breathe,
words battling perpetual conflict against ingrained racism.

I can't breathe,
words demanding justice of equality without concession.

I can't breathe,
words formenting initiation for immediate radical change.

I can't breathe,
words signifying unreserved, courageous collected unity.

I can't breathe,
words altering perspectives between black and white.

I can't breathe,
words constructing the beauty of achieved triumph.

I can't breathe,
the final words of state-sponsored
murder victim the honoured George Floyd.

(For George Floyd)

I can't Breathe 2

"I can't breathe," he gasps in fear and humiliation as a white police officer conditioned by racial bigotry, inbred superiority and emotional indifference chokes the life of a man born with brown skin.

I can't breathe,
words screaming condemnation at blatant, systematic murder.

I can't breathe,
words battering societal walls built upon patent, militant racism.

I can't breathe,
words charging against legalised, lethal action targeting ethnicity.

I can' breathe,
words exposing evil intent, authority utilises to threaten humanity.

I can't breathe,
words taunting warped attitudes sculptured by immoral convictions.

I can't breathe,
words shooting indelible shame through complicitous callous hearts.

I can't breathe,
words taking a fighting stand to change widespread poisoned minds.

I can't breathe,
words seeking unfettered, merciful forbearance that eradicate division.

I can't breathe,
words displaying how beautiful hope blossoms amid enduring strife.

"I can't breathe," he says, as the killing of another black man feels like state-sanctioned practice in order to instil and maintain brutal control.

I can't breathe,
words never to be diminished or forgotten.

(For George Floyd)

British Society

Armed police, persecuted prisoners', predatory paedophiles, enslaved prostitutes,
impoverished pensioners, single parents.

CCTV surveillance, stop and search, paranoid suspicions, suppressive security,
intrusive supervision, zero-tolerance standards.

Political tyrants, governmental thieves, drug traffickers, criminal travellers,
troubled teachers, runaway teenagers, persistent truants, abused toddlers.

Dangerous overcrowded prisons, repressive psychiatric hospitals, neglected
council estates, precarious private housing, shabby benefit hotels, exploitative
homeless hostels, broken family homes, territorial urban streets.

Islamic fundamentalists, underworld crime bosses, youth gang culture,
unsupervised volatile schizophrenics, bigoted impervious judges,
callous greedy landlords, hypocritical Christian preachers, inept foreign
doctors, incompetent social workers.

Unregistered immigrants, disappearing overseas students, illegal workers,
xenophobic activists' groups, Neighbourhood Watch, undercover informers.

British society at its best; disguised as a democracy but in reality a subtle police state
run by a network of powerful, indistinguishable types whose model serves the gifted few.

Aylan

Aylan,
three-year-old boy washed up on a Turkish shore,

Aylan,
Bodrum beach grips a dead toddler in death's claw.

Aylan,
tiny child lies face down wearing a bright, red T-shirt,

Aylan,
media images spark global outrage in desperate alert.

Aylan,
migrant parents' dingy struck by huge Aegean waves,

Aylan,
The capsized vessel throws close family to lost graves.

Aylan,
Greek island of Kos signalled parties' happy salvation,

Aylan,
stormy seas end frightened souls' intended destination.

Aylan,
young father struggles to hold two sons in painful arms,

Aylan,
all staying just afloat in russet waters menacing charms.

Aylan,
barely audible childrens' screams as fatigue takes its toll,

Aylan,
dad's release of Gulap and Aylan as feared monsters' roll.

Aylan,
his wife Rehanna seen 'Floating like a lost balloon' nearby,

Aylan,
only the infant's daddy Abdullah survives as our hearts die.
**(For Aylan and Gulap Kurdi) Ali Hoca Point beach Bodrum
Turkey forever tarnished.**

Justice

Is
there
active,
impartial
and
professional
justice
alive
in
the
English
judiciary
today?

Are
legal
minds
interested
in
establishing
rightful
justice
to
the
upright?

Or
is
it
just
a
game
for
them,
even
if
truth
is

of
indubitable
clarity?

Lives
have
been
irrevocably
changed
beyond
renewal
by
the
judiciary.

Police

Police
brutality
breeds
mob
mentality,
violent
police
collusion
annihilates
public
faith
and
high,
valued
expectation.

How
can
ordinary
people
change
the
system's
legitimate
tool
used
for
silencing
dissenting
voices
and
disagreeable
conduct,
through
barbarity
and
death?

Television

Television the modern-day propaganda tool
a flat-screen situated in every household room.
It will inform you how to think, act and be,
put your feet up and enjoy watching TV.
Let me hypnotise you with lies,
your life's not your own surprise.
You must wear a distinct fashion
and look the part of a trendsetter.
Advertisement design for the gullible.
Television will feed by stealth illusions
and use subtle ploys to breed confusion.
It is insidious brainwashing on a mass scale.
Television has a purpose to misdirect and effect,
as you flick through a multitude of channels trying
to find something worthwhile watching that inevitably
changes your emotions depending on the programme contents.
Television's objective is to mislead and deceive so you can believe.
It remains the one medium powerful enough to subliminally control
you.
Who is watching who?

Television News

Television news has an expiration date
and it fast approaches when our pixel flat-screens
broadcast bloody images too gruesome worth watching.
There is only so much death a Western audience can handle
before flicking for another channel with the digital remote control.
A mother cradling a limp child's corpse in her arms wailing as frightened
and angry people stand around her in an Arab country nobody could find on a map.
A little later on pictures of masked gunmen marching through dusty, ramshackle streets
displaying the strength of a terrorist organisation and swearing revenge tell another story.

January's Shadow of Death

Sleeping upon a concrete stairwell
in temperatures well below zero, lies
an individual wanting to disengage from
secular society through choice, but not sure
whether the luxury of financial abandonment
will allow him wholeheartedly to leave everything
that forms the intrinsic core guiding all the beauty inside.

During one early morning a security officer found his body
stiff and frozen beneath a thin, tatty sleeping-bag incapable of
keeping out Siberian winter weather striking London always after
Christmas, nobody seems prepared for or expects, even when media
outlets like television, radio, and daily newspapers announce the risks
such arctic conditions pose to those of a homeless, elderly, or fragile
nature.

Where Now?

Where now in another repetitious year
tarnished by the blooding, bloody thoughts of destitute striving?
A time vacuum stretches further than imagination can comprehend,
leaving restless resentment to thwart dared-for-expected prosperity.

Unable to initiate a radical change in present circumstances,
it feels, at times, like a situation will lead to drastic measures
that may not bring about a propitious, sagacious outcome
or savoured peaceful resilience.

Suicide

Suicide,
fatalistic, diminishing light,

suicide,
impetuous, consigned right.

Suicide,
frightened, consuming belief,

suicide,
obsessed, incapacitating thief.

Suicide,
planned, murderous exercise,

suicide,
unforgivable, cruel goodbyes.

Suicide,
signalled warnings ignored,

suicide,
emotional pleading deplored.

Suicide,
indifference overriding concern,

suicide,
compassionate feelings adjourn.

Suicide,
brutalised, fulfilment enacted,

suicide,
considered rational deducted.

Suicide,
unpredicted, tortuous affirmation,

suicide,
impotent, destructive captivation.

Suicide.
(For Lance)

I loved my Father

I did love my father.
I loved him more than he knew,
even though there were times my hatred
would for the man explode like a volcano,

resulting in me punching bedroom walls
and breaking my punk records out of impotence
to get back at him, after he had just given me a good-hiding.

I loved my father,
despite our conflicting interests
and his steadfast refusal to fulfil my selfish whims,
especially when friends seemed to possess everything I wanted.

I loved my father,
even though I could not express or emotionalise
my feelings for him in those immature, delinquent, youthful years.

I loved my father,
even though he was older than other dads
and could not play football, his intellect and wisdom
more than made up for that missed pastime of yearning.

I loved my father,
even though he never owned a car,
a house or held a large amount of money in the bank,
I still loved him.

My mother never thought I felt anything for him,
but I put this down to her lack of love and trust in the husband
who had literally rescued her from the unchristian hands of her own
father.

I loved my father,
when the police knocked at the front door
to convey their condolences to my unsurprised mother
when a soldier of honour had passed in to welcomed eternity.

I love my father,
even more now he has gone
and all that remains are fractured memories of days
that never aspired to the beckoning potential always there.

I love my father,
and I wish I could make him feel proud of a son
he only knew for his rebellious mockery and unaffectionate heart.

God bless you dad.

My Father said...

The other night I saw my father
for the first time in thirty years,
when he appeared to me in a dream
and his image left me traumatised.

His body was emaciated, his face gaunt,
his once handsome features shaped by death
but his eyes dazzled with intensity.

I remember they burnt with grave concern
when they looked into mine as dad's familiar voice said
'Son, I've been in a maximum security prison
for the last thirty years'.

Desperation clung to every word dad spoke
during those early hours as he stood
in front of me a mere shadow of himself.

Instinct told me dad needed help
and saw me as his only hope for release
despite the unseen barrier between us.

I felt an urgent desire to save my father
from further the pain and suffering
he had endured for so long.

Dad must have known I had always
compared prison to hell when I thought
about the meaning of the dream later.

I pray his spirit is not there.

God bless you dad.

Inhaling the sea

Inhaling the sea,
beneath maroon rays casting diamond light over easy-minded families
at play.

Inhaling the sea,
feeling beautiful comfort insert wellbeing to inspire this different,
friendly June day.

Inhaling the sea,
a companionable breeze whispers serenity along a coastal city's
shingled shoreline.

Inhaling the sea,
the late hazy afternoon engenders distant childhood recollections of
an era I pine.

Inhaling the sea,
my eight-year-old daughter gathers ocean-washed pebbles in a bucket
to take home.

Inhaling the sea,
petrol coloured waves crash inches from our running feet creating
frothy bubbly foam.

Inhaling the sea,
we clamber across a beach's russet stony baubles enticed by dazzling
Brighton Pier.

Inhaling the sea,
iridescent funfair attractions sparkle juvenile-like thoughts leaving
intentions clear.

Inhaling the sea,

two adventurers spring onto a noisy boardwalk anticipating each exciting ride.

Inhaling the sea,

stopping to buy freshly-made, overpriced sugar doughnuts above a rising dark tide.

Inhaling the sea,

awaiting us are thrill-inducing amusements designed for all captive precious age.

Inhaling the sea,

when starry night gradually arrives realisation signals our final closing, happy stage.

Inhaling the sea.

Revisited

Revisited,
warm childhood memories abound,

revisited,
seaside town's familiarity unfound.

Revisited,
1970's distant forgotten past,

revisited,
2024's rapid futuristic blast.

Revisited,
family daytrips, yearly treat,

revisited,
parent's efforts significant feat.

Revisited,
first positive sight dispelled,

revisited,
innocent halcyon days repelled.

Revisited,
corporate modernity's pervasive facade,

revisited,
fond recollections struck hard.

Revisited,
wandering tawdry streets disengaged,

revisited,
generationally lost and aged.

Revisited,
well-trodden, seasonally reflective pier,

revisited,
old resort's love died here.

Tiannah 2 (Daughter of Truth)

Tiannah,
child of precocious gift,
a super imitator and intelligent creative reality.

Tiannah,
child of refined competence,
a fast leaner and loving social entity.

Tiannah,
child of acute insight,
a natural comprehension and strong bold confidence.

Tiannah,
child of angular beauty,
a delicate touch and pervasive admirable resilience.

Tiannah,
child of trustful inclination,
a content disposition and joyous inspirational sight.

Tiannah,
child of blessed appreciation,
consecrated spirit and unrivalled holy delight.

Tiannah (My only Daughter of Chance)

Tiannah,
now you live and breathe,
it is joyous to watch your development
through innocent childhood towards adolescence
where unknown aspirations sculpture promised years.

Nothing instilled by your loving parents
can really influence what germinates within,
and our expectations mean little if goals you
want accomplished are not brought to fruition.

All your father and mother are enabled to do
is encourage, provide, listen and advise when appropriate.

Your wellbeing and fulfilment is our only concern.

The Poet

I'm a poet
lost for words, bereft of inspiration,
cursing his pen, drowning in frustration
while staring hard at the blank lined page
in the festering state of uncontrollable rage.

I'm a poet
doubting my ability, wanting to create,
yearning for ideas, knowing it's fate
I will never produce beautiful poetry from my soul
as I scream in despair before losing control.

I'm a poet
broken by inarticulacy, spent of creativity,
crying for revelation, abandoning all determination
as I stab my pen into the taunting white sheet
before ripping it to pieces in bitter defeat.

I'm a poet.

The Poet 2

I'm a poet
Living on the street, broken by destitution,
begging for money, receiving no restitution
now cursing at everybody within my scope
knowing I crawl in shit daily, crushed of hope.

I'm a poet
unable to think, hating my plight,
bent on hurting, desperate for flight
away from the bitter environs of my cage
as this deadening hell destroys promised stage.

I'm a poet
shorn of chance, ignored with distain,
screaming in outbursts, mocked in pain
and impotent to change circumstance anytime
because to experience something good would be a crime.

I'm a poet.

BV - #0020 - 060824 - C0 - 216/138/3 - PB - 9781917061100 - Gloss Lamination